Tea-caddy with view of Cobham Hall on lid, stickware caddy ladle, two kettle holders (strips of wood on flexible leather backing), nutmeg grater, cake basket and crumb brush.

TUNBRIDGE WARE

Margaret A. V. Gill

Shire Publications Ltd

CONTENTS

Published in 1997 by Shire Publications Ltd,
Cromwell House, Church Street, Princes Risborough,
Buckinghamshire HP27 9AA, UK.
Copyright © 1985 by Margaret A. V. Gill (text) and
Tunbridge Wells Museum and Art Gallery (photographs). First published 1985; reprinted 1990 and
1997. Shire Album 130. ISBN 0 85263 712 8.

Printed in Great Britain by CIT Printing Services, Press Buildings, Merlins Bridge,
Haverfordwest, Pembrokeshire SA61 1XF.

ACKNOWLEDGEMENTS
    Nearly all the material illustrated in this book forms part of the permanent collection of
Tunbridge Wells Museum and Art Gallery. The trade card on page 4 is from the Banks
Collection and reproduced by courtesy of the Trustees of the British Museum. The publishers acknowledge the assistance of Dr Michael Rowlands of Tunbridge Wells Museum and
Art Gallery in the preparation of this reprint.

British Library Cataloguing in Publication Data. Gill, Margaret A. V. Tunbridge Ware. –
(Shire albums; 130) 1. Tunbridge ware I. Title 745.51 NK9744.T8 ISBN 0-85263-712-8.

*Photograph of Richard J. Sharvill, bandmaker to the firm of Boyce, Brown & Kemp,
selecting slices for assembly into first-stage blocks. He appears to be working direct from a
painted chart for floral banding in standard mosaic.*

Various tools used in the manufacture of Tunbridge ware: hand-operated slitting saw and lathe tools from the workshop of Edmund Nye, toothing plane used by Richard Kemp of Boyce, Brown & Kemp, jack plane and marking gauge.

INTRODUCTION

Were this manufacture smuggled abroad and then imported as a foreign commodity, I am persuaded the people would run after it – but alas everybody knows that it is English and the encouragement is therefore poor. (Samuel Derrick, 1762.)

The term 'Tunbridge ware' has been applied to various types of woodwork during the last three centuries or so, though recently it has become synonymous with the form of mosaic decoration developed in the late 1820s. Long before the introduction of the mosaic technique, however, Tunbridge ware was recognised as a distinctive form of treen. Originally produced by craftsmen for sale at Tunbridge Wells, Kent, by the end of the seventeenth century it was an accepted term requiring no detailed description to be generally understood; nor were its manufacturers confined to the eponymous area, but worked as far afield as London.

The origin of the ware is uncertain, a subject of legend and speculation. Abundant woodlands in the vicinity encouraged cabinet making and turnery to be practised for many years before the skills and refinements of local craftsmen received popular acclaim. The humble origins seem to predate the discovery of the chalybeate springs in 1606, whose exploitation brought into being the nearby town of Tunbridge Wells and provided a new market for local (and London) craftsmen. One version of the discovery explains how Lord North, chancing upon a spring in the forest near Eridge and noting the resemblance of the metallic scum floating on the surface to the medicinal waters of Spa, 'ordered one of his attendants to borrow a little vessel from the neighbouring hovel, that he might taste it'. If the account is accurate, that simple wooden bowl, surely of local manufacture, is one of the earliest examples of Tunbridge ware documented, although the term did not come into use until craftsmen turned their attention to supplying souvenirs for visitors to the new spa.

3

However, none of the manufacturers claimed so early a date for the beginnings of Tunbridge ware. The last firm to operate in Tunbridge Wells maintained they were following a trade established in 1629, but the advertisement indicated neither the source of this statement nor the location of the original establishment. Though ultimately Tunbridge Wells became the principal centre of manufacture, at this time there were no buildings on the site other than the dipper's lodge and perhaps one or two woodmen's cottages. Turned bowls and drinking cups for the use of visitors to the springs may have been made here, or in the nearby communities of Speldhurst and Tonbridge.

Written in the 1830s, Colbran's *New Guide for Tunbridge Wells* recounts the tradition (probably derived from the Burrows family) that Tunbridge ware was first made at Speldhurst, 'and such was the intense interest created by its appearance, that persons, to make themselves acquainted with the secret of manufacturing the ware, used to crawl up the thatched roof, and making a hole in it, looked down upon the workmen. At this time the manufacturer's art was chiefly confined to the making of humming tops and small turnery ware, yet such was the reputation they obtained from their novelty, that when half a dozen tops were made, the parties making them trudged to London to dispose of their ware, and realized from their sale a handsome profit.' No precise date is given, but by implication this must refer to the second or third quarter of the seventeenth century, before any shops had been built at the Wells, for the writer continues with the comment that the manufacturers 'also made their appearance regularly at the steps round the springs, where the country people attended with their vegetables, &c'. Up to about 1830 some London manufacturers also called their work Tunbridge ware and made it available for sale at the Wells.

Another traditional date for the birth of the industry is 1685, two years before the present Pantiles colonnade was built, providing shops for the sale of souvenirs. At whatever date the early turners and cabinet makers started their craft to cater for local needs, or adapted and refined their skills to appeal to gentry and nobility visiting the Wells, by the end of the seventeenth century Tunbridge ware was famous. As a result of royal patronage, first by Queen Henrietta Maria in 1630 and then by Charles II and his consort after the Restoration, the Wells had become so popular a resort that tradesmen constructed booths beneath the trees from which to sell their wares, and later permanent shops. When Celia Fiennes, that connoisseur of spas, visited the Wells in 1697 she found a row of shops along one side of the Walke 'full of all sorts of toys, silver, china, milliners, and all sorts of curious woodenware, which this place is noted for (the delicate, neate and thin ware of wood, both white and lignum vitae wood)'.

Detail from the trade card of Morris's Tunbridge Ware Manufactory, Trafalgar Place, Brighton, about 1815. (Left) A turner standing at a treadle-driven lathe with chisels, gouges and other tools on the bench and wall rack. (Right) Cabinet makers producing boxes at the work-bench.

Trade lists showing the range of larger articles made by John Robinson and referring to the 'great assortment of Tunbridge Toys and every kind of Turnery-Ware, made to any Pattern, for Exportation, or Home Consumption'. The complete catalogue is that published in 1795; the detail (right) comes from a similar 1797 list also printed by Jasper Sprange, in which Robinson describes himself as Tunbridge ware manufacturer, print-seller and perfumer, of Piccadilly and the Parade, Tunbridge Wells.

EIGHTEENTH-CENTURY TUNBRIDGE WARE

*Wit must seem flat, and Sense but heavy
 Stuff
To noddles cramm'd with Dighton's mus-
 ty Snuff
Whose nicer tastes think Wit consists
 alone
In Tunbridge Wooden Box with Wooden
 Spoon.* (Thomas Baker, 1706.)

The earliest Tunbridge ware is difficult to identify, as it seems to have been distinguished from treen made in other parts of England only by the neater manner of its manufacture. By some the term was limited to turnery, but even in the seventeenth century Tonbridge craftsmen were producing fine joinery such as backgammon boards; by the eighteenth century the industry was well established and an increasing range of articles was marketed. Contemporary references are unfortunately few. Howev-er, Mrs Pendarves wrote of 'Tunbridge voiders' (1727) and Mrs Elizabeth Mon-tagu took the liberty of sending the Duchess of Portland Tunbridge ware churns, butter prints and skimming dishes for her dairy (1745). Samuel Derrick presented the daughters of an acquaint-ance with a dressing glass and a set of toilette boxes 'together with the prettiest tea-chest I could lay my hands upon . . . these, as well as many other useful things, and some of the most curious toys I ever saw, are said to be the manufacture of the

LEFT: *Late Georgian snuff or tobacco box with inlaid lid, the sides of each fan and scale inlay shaded by scorching.*

RIGHT: *Detail shows similar scorching on the scalloped border on the lid of an octagonal work-box, whose principal decoration is in half-square mosaic (about 1830).*

place' (1762). Thomas Benge Burr, in the first history of Tunbridge Wells, summarised the local trade as consisting of 'a variety of toys in wood, such as tea-chests, dressing boxes, snuff-boxes, punch-ladles, and numerous other little articles of the same kind' (1766). Among the smaller items were probably 'minia-

ture tea-sets, nattily turned out of native yew wood', which as late as the 1880s were 'still a Tunbridge Wells speciality'.

The industry was based on the use of local woods, and this continued throughout the eighteenth century. Derrick made particular note of yew, cherry and holly, Burr recorded that 'besides holly, they

Late Georgian cribbage board with ivory inlays and bandings of mixed exotic and native woods, including red and black ebony and green oak. The small pieces of veneer were not cut or mounted individually but made as strips. First a laminated block composed of slices of different coloured woods of varying thickness was sawn into several sub-blocks each the width of the banding; from these were cut the veneer strips — a simple sort of mass production! To achieve the oblique banding, sub-blocks were sawn from the main block at an angle.

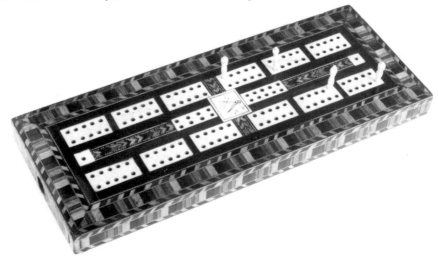

ABOVE: *Late Georgian box with cube pattern and vandykes in a variety of native woods with a wide range of texture and markings. The tea-caddy is an unusual specimen as only three woods have been used for the fine cube pattern, including the rare green. It was probably made by Wise of Tonbridge, from whose descendants the caddy was acquired. Cube pattern became popular towards the end of the eighteenth century and continued until Tunbridge ware ceased to be manufactured in the 1930s. On earlier examples it was the sole decoration or combined with simple stringing or vandykes; later more elaborate geometric or floral banding in mosaic was added except on very small articles.*

BELOW: *Early nineteenth-century work-box with engraving of Tonbridge Castle inside lid (probably by Wise) and mid nineteenth-century book-rest with floral banding by Nye or Barton. In the earliest examples of cube pattern (and the work of certain later manufacturers) the lozenge-shaped pieces of veneer were applied individually; later, complete panels of patterned veneer were often used. To produce these, sticks of lozenge section (A) were glued together in bundles of three (B) and these were assembled to form larger blocks (C); finally triangular sticks were inserted along the irregular sides with plain strips to hold the block secure and form a border. Dependent on the length of the stick, sixty or so identical veneers (D) came from the workshop of Thomas Green of Rye. The fragment at the front (E) is the finest gauge of cube pattern ever produced in Tunbridge ware, the sides of the lozenges measuring only 2.5mm.*

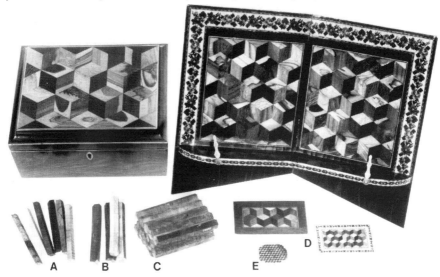

7

use no small quantity of cherry-tree, plum-tree, yew and sycamore', while Hasted in his history of Kent mentioned beech and sycamore as the woods principally used 'with yew and holly inlaid' (1778). At the end of the previous century Celia Fiennes had noted wares of both white wood and the darker foreign lignum vitae. She is probably correct in ascribing both wares to the local craftsmen, but in the trade only the former seems to have been regarded as Tunbridge ware, for in their advertisements and trade cards eighteenth-century turners usually list both lignum vitae and Tunbridge wares.

In catering for the fashionable visitors from the capital, the Kentish craftsmen were quick to adapt themselves to any new technique of decoration that might appeal. It is evident from contemporary descriptions, workshop tradition and actual examples of wood wares preserved by descendants of the early manufacturers that several different techniques were used in the eighteenth century. Derrick thought 'the inlaying and veneering very beautiful'; Burr commented on the use of holly 'which grows in great abundance in the surrounding country and furnishes a prodigious variety of the prettiest ornamental inlays that can be imagined, some of which are so excellent in their kind, that it is hard to believe they are not assisted by the pencil'. As well as marquetry in naturally contrasting woods, white woods such as holly were scorched or stained to give the effect of shading on individual pieces of veneer; such inlays of shell design, said to have been obtained from London, were used as centres, as also were stained or painted floral motifs. Scorching by means of hot sand over a wider surface produced an imitation of tortoiseshell. Another type of inlay consisted of banding with an oblique pattern resembling twisted rope. Towards the end of the century the cube pattern, an all-over parquetry design giving the optical illusion of three dimensions, became popular, sometimes combined with vandyke edging. Painted wares were also produced, some of which had additional decoration in the form of printed labels or engravings.

Eighteenth-century 'japanned' ware, probably from Wise's Manufactory, the handled work-box and dome-lidded caddy having been acquired from the Wise family. A note in George Wise's handwriting, dated 1st January 1868 and bequeathing the latter to his daughter, describes it as 'The Painted round top small Tea cady Black & White painted by Mr. Connard'. Its inner lid is mottled, perhaps in imitation of the tortoiseshell effect normally produced by scorching with hot sand. The theme on the card-box in the centre is unusual in drawing its inspiration from India rather than China.

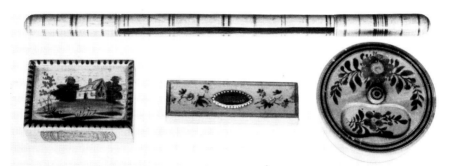

Late Georgian painted ware: (Top) Knitting case with red, black and yellow bands. (Left) Cottage design on sliding lid of box, with printed paper label on side 'A Present from Oxford'. (Centre) Box with rose pattern and enamelled plaque 'A Tunbridge Wells Gift'. (Right) Snuff box, with pivot lid and kidney-shaped aperture for insertion of thumb and finger; floral decoration in blue and green, in addition to red and black lines.

PAINTED AND PRINTED WARES

Wanted a Man and a Boy in the Tunbridge-ware Line — The Man will be required to make White Wood Boxes in the best manner for Ladies to paint on; the Boy to make Sliding, Puzzle Boxes and other small Articles: and both may have constant employment. (Maidstone Journal, 27th February 1810.)

Simple turnery and other plain wares continued to be produced throughout the eighteenth century and into the nineteenth, though some was intended to receive the customer's own decoration, as the advertisement in the *Maidstone Journal* indicates. The rest was painted at the manufactories using various techniques.

In Georgian times and well into the Regency period a type of japanned ware was made; it was not true japanning but a black paint and varnish applied as a background on white wood, leaving the design in reserve. Some of this seems to have been inspired by contemporary marquetry, as for example the floral pattern on the work basket made by Wise; other designs were influenced by the fashion for oriental art, though English country scenes were also depicted.

Other painted wares were in colour against the light wood background, the simplest consisting merely of narrow red and black bands, sometimes with green or yellow, the more ornate having polychrome floral patterns, landscapes and castles or cottages. These latter were often painted round the sides of turned articles so that the objects themselves became model buildings.

Painting was also combined with other forms of decoration, enamelled porcelain plaques, paper labels and engravings. The labels might be printed with either an appropriate line or verse, for example 'Remember the giver', 'Tho' absent, not forgotten', 'As the rose, so is life', 'A token of friendship', 'Within this Box/ You there may see,/The face of one/ That's dear to me', or with a souvenir inscription, such as 'A trifle from Bath', 'A present from Gravesend', 'A gift from Hothampton'. The above are a selection of labels produced by Jasper Sprange's printing office in Tunbridge Wells during the 1790s for local Tunbridge ware manufacturers, who were making souvenir wares for many other resorts.

Many of the engravings used were printed by the Wises of Tonbridge, some specially designed for this purpose, and, like the printed labels, the views include Brighton, Margate and other resorts. Usually hand-coloured, the prints were pasted on to light wood, often in com-

9

BELOW: *Face screen, bearing rubber-stamped mark of Thomas Barton, dating from the last quarter of the nineteenth century. The stand is painted with red, black and green lines, the screen colour-printed with typical Barton design of goldfinches at their nest on an apple branch.*

ABOVE: *Early nineteenth-century octagonal games-box with simple inlaid border and octagonal paper panel bearing hand-coloured pen and ink drawing on lid. On the central card, the ace of spades is shown with the duty mark and a mixture of legible and imitation lettering; the former includes the Garter motto, 'G III REX' either side of the crown and 'I.J. & A. SHARP. TUNB. WELLS' beneath. A similar design also occurs as an engraving, the Sharp family being both printers and Tunbridge ware manufacturers. As early as 1808 they had a manufactory at the back of Culverden Row and later another at Oldenburgh House at the top of London Road.*

bination with painted decoration, simple lines, flowers, japanned banding and imitations of inlaid vandykes, geometric borders and rosewood veneer; sometimes the inlaid patterns and panels of veneer were genuine. To protect the surface of the engraving, the paper was varnished. Beginning in the eighteenth century, the printed wares were popular during the Regency period, probably declining with the introduction of mosaic ware.

Following that decline, the technique was not completely forgotten, being revived for such articles as stamp boxes, on to whose lids were stuck either prints or actual stamps. Postcard boxes also occasionally had a printed label, and one manufacturer in addition to mosaic de-

coration applied photographic prints (mainly views of the Isle of Wight).

From the 1870s onwards another form of printed ware, known as Decalcomanie, was produced by Thomas Barton; in contrast to the earlier wares, the designs were printed in gummy colours on tissue paper and then transferred directly on to the wood. In this he may have been influenced by the monochrome Mauchline ware, as he is said to have experimented with fern pattern ware (another type produced by the Scottish souvenir industry). At this time Henry Hollamby also advertised 'grey and white wood articles for painting, fern printing, &c, &c'.

LEFT: *Regency column spice container of sycamore, each box individually marked with printed scroll label. Amongst the 1790s proofs from Jasper Sprange's Printing Office are two sets of plain spice labels (listing CINNAMON, MACE, CLOVES, NUTMEGS, GINGER, ALLSPICE and PEPPER), one of which may have been printed for John Robinson.*
RIGHT: *Regency Pope Joan board with hand-coloured engravings and simple painted banding.*

BELOW: *Regency work-box with hand-coloured engraving of 'The Promenade & Pump Room, Cheltenham, Published at Wises Manufactory, Tunbridge Town' mounted in centre of lid. The rest of the box is painted with imitation wood veneers and 'japanned' banding.*

11

Triangular sticks, core and glued blocks (one still bound with string) for stickware, and examples of mid nineteenth-century stickware: cylindrical box, caddy ladles and miniature chamber candle-holder.

STICKWARE AND HALF-SQUARE MOSAIC

Mr James Burrows. . . was attracted by a row of wooden beads, worn by a lady, which did not correspond with the colours of her dress; thinking that something of the kind might be effected in Tunbridge ware, of different woods combined, he eventually produced a necklace of the mosaic work . . . This acting as a stimulus upon his inventive faculties, he turned his attention more particularly to the improvement of the ware, and has succeeded, we believe, beyond his most sanguine expectations. (Colbran, 1839.)

In describing the invention of 'mosaic work', Colbran was writing between ten and fifteen years after the event; with so many contemporaries still alive to contradict any errors, he is undoubtedly correct in ascribing the invention to James Burrows. What may be questioned is the general assumption among modern students that the lady's wooden beads inspired Burrows to produce a necklace veneered with minute tesserae of tessellated mosaic ware, or what most people would recognise as 'Tunbridge ware'. More probably the account condenses the development of several years.

Manufacturers were already producing obliquely banded inlays cut from lami- nated blocks and would have been aware of the different patterns that resulted from the turning of naturally banded woods. A string of turned wooden beads of parti-coloured woods could well have suggested to Burrows the possibilities of making regular patterns by turning beads from blocks made up from sticks of contrasting colours (i.e. stickware). By looking at the end of such a block he would have appreciated the other potentials: instead of turning it on the lathe, by sawing across the block he could produce patterned veneers (i.e. half-square mosaic). A desire to introduce representational designs may then have stimulated his inventive faculties to attend to the improvement of the ware (i.e. tessellated mosaic).

Whatever the exact date of its introduction, stickware became popular for smaller turned articles in the late 1820s and continued to be manufactured well into the twentieth century.

To produce stickware, sticks of triangular or lozenge cross-section of contrasting woods were prepared, 6 or 7 inches (150-180 mm) in length. These were grouped to form circular bundles, then glued together using wet string

ABOVE: *Writing cabinet of 1830s, sides, doors and central panel of top decorated in cube pattern, other surfaces with half-square mosaic.*

BELOW: *(Lower left) Small stick mosaic box, mid nineteenth century. The patterns on the lid and base are not veneers, but were cut from a solid section of patterned block, the interior hollowed and the sides turned as in stickware. (Upper left) Box decorated with veneer cut from similar block, made up from plain lozenge and half-square and patterned triangular sticks. (Centre) Rectangular, square and triangular patterned sticks. (Right) Ends of blocks and veneer with similar pattern elements.*

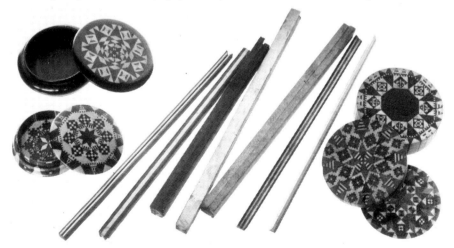

Half-square mosaic of the 1830s. (Left) Tea-caddy, with bird and inscription 'A Present from Tunbridge Wells' in early tessellated mosaic. (Upper right) Tray with cube pattern. (Lower right) Box with character from Chevy Chase in mosaic on lid.

bound tightly round to hold them all in place while the animal glue dried. With larger blocks, concentric rings of sticks were built up in layers. Often there was an octagonal core of plain wood in the centre; this might either be removed at a later stage for hollow wares or its end might be concealed with a patterned veneer. When these cylindrical blocks were turned on the lathe, the characteristic curvilinear patterns of stickware were effected by the uneven depth of penetration of the moulding.

Half-square mosaic was made in a similar way, the sticks usually being of half-square or square section; and a related type of stick mosaic used also triangular, lozenge and rectangular sticks. At quite an early stage in its development patterned sticks were used, made by oblique cutting of laminated blocks. As with stickware, bundles of sticks were glued together, but with an eye to the pattern at the end of the block, for the veneers were cut across the pattern. For half-square mosaic the blocks were usually square or rectangular in section; for other stick mosaics, the block was often circular so that either it could be cut into veneers across the pattern or its sides could be turned to produce stickwork.

TESSELLATED MOSAIC

Such is the value set upon Tunbridge-ware articles, that few persons visit the place without purchasing for their friends some reminiscence of it. (Colbran, 1839.)

Regarded by many as Tunbridge ware *par excellence*, the tessellated mosaic technique seems to have been invented by James Burrows in the late 1820s. The decoration, consisting of inlaid panels and bandings with patterns and representational designs executed in tessellated wood, gives the appearance of true mosaic, but the apparent intricacy of the work is deceptive. The minute tesserae were neither cut nor inlaid separately and, though requiring precision at all stages, the process of making a mosaic veneer was quite simple.

First a basic motif was selected, a suitable published picture or one specially designed; this was redrawn on graph paper in polychrome, the design translated into squares as on contemporary

14

ABOVE: *Early mosaic panels with the complete background as well as the subject worked in tesserae. (Left) Book-rest, combining a tessellated mosaic bird with a border of elaborate half-square mosaic. (Upper right) Tea-caddy with butterfly and dog, probably by Burrows. (Lower right) Box with design of girl on donkey holding a parasol (probably Princess Victoria).*

RIGHT, UPPER: *Berlin woolwork patterns from Nye's Manufactory with the mosaic veneer based on them. Woolwork designs were first published in Germany at the beginning of the nineteenth century but only became popular in the 1830s, coinciding with the development of Tunbridge ware mosaic.*

RIGHT, LOWER: *Design from Nye's Manufactory, probably by Thomas Barton in the 1850s. Ostensibly designed for marquetry, examples of veneers exist showing it in standard mosaic.*

embroidery pattern sheets. Alternatively an actual Berlin woolwork pattern might be used. In some cases the craftsman worked directly from such a pattern, in others more detailed instructions were devised. These took the form either of line by line lists of the woods required, or of an enlarged chart on which each square was marked with a key letter indicating the appropriate wood.

Meanwhile wood slices had been prepared. Tunbridge ware manufacturers

April 6th 1842

Woods for Scroll, without the Center

1   5 Holly, 1 Fustic 1 Holly, 1 Fustic 1 Purple
    1 Black, 2 Holly, 1 Black, 1 Holly

2   1 Holly, 1 Plum, 3 Cherry, 3 Holly, 1 Purple, 1 Fus
    tick 2 Purple, 1 Black 1 Holly, 1 Black, 1 Part
    ridge, 1 Black,

3   2 Holly, 3 Plum, 1 Cherry, 1 Holly, 1 Red, 1 Holly
    2 Purple, 4 Black, 2 Holly, 3 Partridge

4   3 Holly, 1 Plum, 1 Red, 1 Plum, 1 Holly, 2 Red
    5 Holly, 1 Partridge 1 Lab.. 1 Partridge

5   3 Holly, 1 Cherry, 1 Plum, 1 Red, 1 Plum, 1 Red
    2 Plum, 4 Holly, 3 Laburnum,

6   3 Holly, 2 Cherry, 1 Plum, 1 Red, 3 Plum
    4 Holly, 1 Lab.. 1 Barbery, 1 Lab..

7   4 Holly, 1 Cherry, 1 Plum, 1 Rose 1 Red, 1 Plum
    1 Red, 4 Holly, 1 Barbery, 1 Black, 1 Barbery

8   5 Holly, 1 Plum, 1 Rose 3 Red, 4 Holly, 1 Black
    1 Green, 1 Black

LEFT: *Instructions for making a border pattern dated 6th April 1842, consisting of four pages of line by line lists of the wood slices required with the number of each type totalled at the end: holly 550, fustick 35, purple 60, rose 56, black 54, plum 80, cherry 35, partridge 6, bar 103, laburnum 6, barberry 29, green 57, acacia 6, orange 13, yew 19.*

BELOW: *Two charts for leafy scroll patterns. (Left) With background summarised as lines. (Right) With individual squares of background as well as the motif indicated by code letters.*

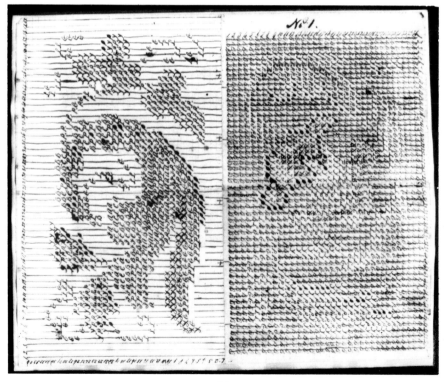

Blocks and slices from the workshop of Thomas Green of Rye. Top row: Wood roughly trimmed ready for sawing into slices; branch of green oak mounted to prevent wastage; bundle of holly strips in storage guards and selection of plain veneers of various woods. Bottom row: Bundle of banded veneer slices tied for storage, and various single banded slices; bundle of slices assembled into parrot motif, between guards in preparation for glueing; two sub-blocks with design of crown and inscription 'G R 1937', intended for coronation of George VI.

prided themselves on using natural woods, though some such as sycamore, maple, holly and satin wood were 'assisted' by soaking in water drawn from the chalybeate spring or by boiling. Even without artificial dyeing a good range of colour was available, including black, red, yellow and green, the last obtained locally from oak (and certain other trees) attacked by the fungus *Chlorosplenium aeruginascens,* which stained the tissues a brilliant emerald. In the 1840s manufacturers had a choice of some forty native and foreign woods, by the end of the century well over a hundred, and in the 1920s the Tunbridge Wells Manufacturing Company advertised 'about 180 different woods are used in the mosaics'. By sawing across a block at different angles, certain woods such as palmyra yielded several different effects, adding to the range, but for normal purposes about thirty kinds of wood were found sufficient.

Having been properly seasoned, the wood was cut into slips of standard size. Their length would determine the number of veneers that might be cut from one pattern block, their width would determine the number of identical pattern blocks that could be produced from that one batch, and their thickness was equal to one square of pattern (or multiple thereof).

With his chart or instruction sheet before him and slips of different coloured woods piled to hand, the bandmaker began with the first column or line of the design. Selecting the correct number and colour of slips, he stacked them in order and bound them together until he had dealt similarly with all the other lines. Then, using hot animal glue, each stack was glued and cramped to squeeze out any surplus; when dry, these first-stage blocks were trimmed, then sawn longitudinally across the laminations to form striped slices with the individual pattern line visible at their ends. One bandmaker reckoned on cutting thirteen slices from a block made of 1 inch (25 mm) slips, but the number would vary according to the gauge of tessera.

Slices from each of these blocks were then assembled and glued to form second-stage blocks with the complete design at the end. These could then be sawn into a series of identical veneers ready for mounting. As all the veneers from one batch of blocks were rarely

Detail from a blotter with a view of Tonbridge Castle in early mosaic showing the technique of oblique cutting (in foreground), angled juxtaposition of sub-blocks (above painted windows to right) and use of shaped elements for special features such as the arched entrance and windows. The border is in developed half-square technique, using square mosaic elements as well as half-square and lozenge. Possibly made by Burrows.

needed immediately, the remainder were stored either as uncut blocks or as a stack of veneer slices tied between stiff guards to prevent warping or sometimes supported individually with paper pasted on to one surface.

There were variants to this basic method. Where a design was large it was made up in sections, and second-stage sub-blocks were glued together to form the large pattern block. Where several squares of the same colour came together in one line of the pattern, slices of the thickness of two or more squares might be used instead of several standard slices; this resulted in a rectangular tessera appearing in the completed mosaic. Where a design was of irregular outline coarse slips of wood were set round the edge to support it and were only removed at the final stage when the veneer was about to be mounted. Sometimes, as well as the central panel of mosaic, the background and banding were incorporated as part of a single veneer by the addition of plain or patterned slices to the second-stage block; this method was frequently used for ve-

neers intended for the lids of small boxes.

Size of tessera varies, the majority measuring about 1 millimetre (0.04 inch), but there were a few veneers executed in exceptionally large or small gauge. At the Great Exhibition of 1851 Edmund Nye displayed a table with 'the representation of a vessel sailing on the ocean, which viewed at a distance is a perfect imitation of nature'. The mosaic panel contained 110,800 pieces, each measuring nearly 3 millimetres (0.1 inch). By contrast one of the butterfly panels on the bookstand also in the Exhibition contained thirteen thousand pieces, some scarcely 0.5 millimetre (0.02 inch) in length; this, however, was not standard mosaic but a precise form of marquetry using extremely fine mosaic elements. A fine tessellated mosaic was used for certain matchbox-size subjects, dogs, butterflies and one of the portrait heads of Queen Victoria on the lids of stamp boxes.

Despite certain limitations, the mosaic technique was sufficiently versatile for the execution of a wide range of designs, abstract and representational. The abstract vary from simple banding to quite complex motifs, inspired by or adapted from Berlin woolwork patterns. Probably the largest group of representational designs are the floral motifs, again mostly derived from embroidery sheets. Among animals, deer, dogs, mice, birds, butterflies, moths, beetles and shells are represented, and there is a rather curious selection of human figures, including St George and the dragon, a girl on a pony, the young Prince of Wales (later Edward VII) with a dog and parrot, a rider from Chevy Chase, other huntsmen and a milkmaid. Another important group is the topographical scenes, intended mostly for the more expensive end of the market. Miscellaneous motifs include the impressive brig at sea, Thomas Barton's design exhibited by Nye at the Great Exhibition and reproduced in the twentieth century by the Tunbridge Wells Manufacturing Company, and the Prince of Wales's feathers, probably introduced in the 1840s to commemorate the birth of Prince Albert Edward and revived in the 1860s to celebrate his marriage. Mosaic was also used for short inscriptions, labelling the intended contents of boxes ('Besique', 'Needles', 'Stamps', 'Gloves') or naming the resort of which the article was to be a souvenir ('A present from Hastings', 'Rye', 'Killarney Lakes').

TOPOGRAPHICAL VIEWS IN MOSAIC WARE

H. H. invites the attention of the Gentry and Visitors of Tunbridge Wells to his large and interesting variety of Mosaics, among which will be found Views of the following places of note: THE PARADE, ERIDGE CASTLE, TUN-BRIDGE CASTLE, PENSHURST PLACE, BATTLE ABBEY, BAYHAM ABBEY, HEVER CASTLE, SHAKESPEARE'S HOUSE, HURSTMONCEUX CASTLE &c., &c., Inlaid and Manufactured into a large and varied assortment of both useful and ornamental articles. (From an advertisement of Henry Hollamby, 1880s.)

Whereas abstract border patterns, floral motifs, dogs, birds and other representational designs were from the first interpreted in tessellated mosaic, only in the mature period was this technique regularly applied to topographical views. In early views several techniques were used;

Panel with a view of Eridge Castle. The inscription on the reverse reads: 'This was the last work made by Mr. Humphrey Burrows the Elder at Jordan Place Tonbridge Wells in the Year 1844.' The block used small sub-blocks of tessellated mosaic of various-sized tesserae set at different angles and with some bands curved; also strips and shaped pieces. This was combined with a marquetry foreground and flag staffs.

ABOVE: *Panel with a view of Windsor Castle bearing a pencilled inscription on the reverse: 'This specimen of gauge work was made at Mr. George Wise's Tunbridge Ware Manufactory, Frant-rd by William Harris Jr.' According to family tradition, this view was on one of the pieces purchased for Princess Victoria in the 1830s.*

BELOW: *Panel with a view of Buckhurst Park near Withyham, the seat of Earl De La Warr, in early style combining tessellated mosaic in the trees and foreground with gauge mosaic for the building.*

BOTTOM: *Engraving of Buckhurst Park by R. W. Smart from Colbran's 'New Guide for Tunbridge Wells' (1840), on which the Tunbridge ware design was based.*

ABOVE: *Thermometer stand by Alfred Talbot and tray with identical scrolling leaf pattern, probably from the same manufacturer.*

BELOW: *Detail of the tray above, showing a view of St Helena Cottage and the outcrop of rocks on Tunbridge Wells Common, with buildings on Mount Ephraim in the background. Several versions of this view based on the same engraving exist, of which this is the finest, combining early tessellated mosaic with larger elements and using the natural grain markings of the woods as well as their colours to indicate variety of texture. Although the final result resembles marquetry, the veneer was cut from a block.*

the influence of marquetry is evident in the division of the design into areas, but instead of cutting single pieces of veneer for inlay the manufacturers constructed blocks for the whole design from which batches of complete veneers could be cut.

The manner in which the small areas of the design were treated varied. One manufacturer composed his pattern block of shaped elements cut from textured mosaic blocks; apart from such details as window mullions, the whole design was in mosaic with the banding of each area variously orientated. Others, in addition to textured mosaic, cut their shaped elements from solid wood, in some cases

LEFT: *Detail of panel with a view of Battle Abbey Gatehouse, in fine gauge work for the building and tessellated mosaic for the tree and foreground. Thomas Barton was awarded first prize for it in the Industrial Exhibition at Tunbridge Wells in 1864.*

BELOW: *Work-box with view of Tonbridge Priory, showing an early and not very successful use of tessellated mosaic. In the foreground and among the ruins are rectangular tesserae.*

The medieval church and Roman lighthouse at Dover on a jewel-box. Like the majority of views in the tessellated mosaic technique, the lay of the tesserae in the building is vertical while that of the foreground is horizontal, which helps create a feeling of perspective. Some of the divisions between sub-blocks are visible.

Watercolour pattern on squared paper for the above view, based on a design predating the restoration of the roof of St Mary's church in the 1860s. This pattern was probably amongst the material acquired by Boyce, Brown & Kemp from Hollamby.

skilfully utilising the natural markings to give extra texture as well as colour to the design.

A refinement of this gauge work was the 'stone for stone' method developed by Thomas Barton at Nye's manufactory. Following a carefully drawn architectural design, each piece was precisely cut to give the impression of perspective; only in the less important parts of the picture such as trees and the foreground was tessellated mosaic used.

Although gauge work was a more rapid process than marquetry, because all the elements of the design were shaped as sticks which were then assembled into blocks from which a batch of complete veneers could be cut, this method required greater skill and more time than tessellated mosaic, so that once satisfactory results could be obtained in mosaic, gauge declined.

The earliest experiments using pure mosaic for topographical scenes were unsatisfactory, partly because such views as the ruins of Tonbridge Priory were rather nebulous in form, but principally because the whole composition was executed with the lines of tesserae running horizontally, resulting in a merging of the main subject with the foreground and a loss of architectural verticals. Once these problems had been overcome by illustrating more distinctive monuments and changing the direction of tesserae from horizontal to vertical for the buildings while retaining horizontal strata for the foregrounds, tessellated mosaic for topographical scenes replaced other techniques.

The majority of mosaic views have shaped outlines, the lower corners simply rounded, the upper edge following the profile of the building and surrounding trees. To protect these edges during manufacture and storage coarse waster pieces were added, which were later cut away when the veneer was inlaid. Three of Hollamby's designs, Shakespeare's House, the Pantiles and Herstmonceux Castle, have regular outlines, with a cloudy sky depicted in mosaic as well as the main scene and foreground.

At least fifty different views appear on Tunbridge ware, of which Eridge Castle, the nearby residence of the Marquess of Abergavenny, was the most popular, followed by Tonbridge Castle and the Pantiles. There were also general views of Tunbridge Wells, buildings patronised by the great such as the Calverley Hotel, picturesque cottages illustrated in guide books such as Farnborough Lodge, romantic ruins such as Bayham Abbey and various country houses in the neighbourhood such as Penshurst Place and Hever Castle. In addition to local scenes, monuments in other areas of tourist resort or popular fame were portrayed: Windsor Castle, Muckross Abbey, Abbotsford, Glena Cottage, Shakespeare's House and the Capitol, the last probably intended for export to the United States.

A half-used block from the workshop of Henry Hollamby depicting Shakespeare's Birthplace, the design based on an early view of the house prior to the demolition of adjacent buildings and restoration of dormer windows in the late 1850s and early 1860s. This view apparently attracted the attention of the Prince of Wales and was much admired at the Bath and West of England Show in 1881.

Marquetry tray, boxes and paper knife made by Robert Russell. Labels on the boxes read 'To H.R.H. The Duchess of Kent. R. Russell, Inventor & Manufacturer of Tunbridge Wells Marquetry, Chapel Place, Tunbridge Wells. N.B. No stained or dyed woods used'. Russell was the only craftsman to produce this type of marquetry; with his death in the early 1870s no more was made.

TUNBRIDGE WELLS MARQUETRY AND OTHER VENEERS

THE TUNBRIDGE WELLS MAR-QUETRY, OR IMPROVED TUN-BRIDGE WARE. ROBERT RUS-SELL, Inventor and Sole Manufacturer of the above Beautiful Wood Work, (analogous to the Tunbridge Ware, but of a superior character,) respectfully informs the Gentry, Nobility, and Inhabitants generally of the Town and Neighbourhood, that after some years close application, he has completed a very large and elegant assortment of articles fit for the Drawing Room, Studio, &c. (Advertisement, 1863.)

Robert Russell's 'improved Tunbridge ware' is immediately recognisable: a distinctive style of marquetry using intricately interlocking elements like an abstract jigsaw puzzle. According to family tradition, his templates were made from ox bone, the only bone from which sufficiently large slips could be cut; finding no tool on the market fine enough for his work, he invented a treadle-operated saw with delicate blades some no more than an inch (25 mm) in length, made out of steel busks from his wife's stays. Each piece of inlay was marked out and cut individually, using furze from the Common or wood from the gardens of local gentry, whose gardeners came to him

with any loppings showing good colour or interesting pattern. Apprenticed in the late 1820s, Russell was probably inspired to develop his own form of marquetry by the atmosphere of experiment that surrounded the introduction of the mosaic technique. He exhibited at the Great Exhibition of 1851, was patronised by royalty and received more orders from America than he could cope with. Requiring time and skill to produce, this type of marquetry was not copied by other Tunbridge ware manufacturers, and being the work of one man relatively little of this ware was made.

Remarkable though the development of mosaic inlay was, it did not oust completely the production of marquetry. The two techniques continued side by side, sometimes even on the same object. However, certain manufacturers particularly excelled in the process, notably Thomas Barton. His cube pattern wares were produced by the marquetry method, as were his traditional floral inlays and the bird studies that are so characteristic of his hand. An impressed contemporary in the 1880s gave an admiring account of his use of veneers: 'Every piece is selected according as the figuring lends itself to a particular shape — say the breast or the wing of a bird, or a leaf or a flower – and the effect is not only telling, but artistic, and exceedingly pretty.'

Another rare form of veneer decoration, certainly made by George Wise and perhaps by other manufacturers for a limited period in the 1830s and 1840s, was produced by rolling and pressing wood shavings with glue into a solid block, which when cut transversely gave veneers of marbled appearance. When applied it was often combined with panels or borders of half-square mosaic, and sometimes with early tessellated mosaic.

LEFT: *Tilt top table of rosewood with Berlin woolwork bandings in mosaic typical of Nye and Barton, and a bullfinch in marquetry designed by Thomas Barton in the 1850s.*

BELOW: *Marbled veneer on a double tea-caddy combined with marquetry star and fans on the lid, and half-square mosaic on interior compartment lids. Probably made by Wise in the 1830s.*

BOTTOM: *Pair of original watercolours painted for Wise and showing his manufactory at Tonbridge and repository at Tunbridge Wells about 1825. They were intended to be reproduced as engravings. Although prints were sold separately, the vandyke border indicates that these were designed for use on Tunbridge ware.*

G. & J. BURROWS,

(*Inventors of the Mosaic Inlaid Ware.*)

PARADE, TUNBRIDGE WELLS,

AND

CULVERDEN COTTAGE, EPHRAIM TERRACE.

Manufacturers of Tunbridge Ware, Wholesale and Retail.

A great assortment of Inlaid Turnery, of the Newest Inventions.

MANUFACTORY, HANOVER ROAD.

LEFT: *Detail from a watercolour by H. Harris, showing the Royal Party with Princess Victoria in front of Humphrey Burrows's Tunbridge Ware Manufactory about 1834.*
RIGHT: *Advertisement of George and James Burrows in Colbran's 'New Guide for Tunbridge Wells' (1840), illustrating their showrooms on the Pantiles (then known as the Parade). The premises were later occupied by Hollamby.*

SOME TUNBRIDGE WARE MANUFACTURERS

WISE

The Wise family business was established at Tonbridge by the first George Wise in 1746. He was succeeded in turn by his son Thomas, Thomas's nephew George Wise Senior, and the latter's son George Wise Junior, who died in 1876. Their premises by the Medway bridge included large workshops and timber sheds for seasoning wood; by the 1820s Wise also had a repository in Tunbridge Wells. Successive generations of Wises produced all the different types of ware, plain turnery, painted and printed (using engravings from their own printing office), scorched inlay and marquetry, and finally stickware and mosaic inlay. It was said that one of the Burrows family's apprentices, having learnt the secret of mosaic manufacture, joined Wise, introducing the new technique. Like several other manufacturers, the Wises were patronised by royalty and exported not only to other parts of England but also to the United States of America.

BURROWS

The Burrows family of Tunbridge Wells were, along with the Wises, one of the earliest specialist manufacturers. The first William Burrows may have acquired Jordan House about 1740 from Mr Jordan, himself said to be a Tunbridge ware maker. Of his grandsons, Humphrey (who enjoyed the patronage of Princess Victoria) managed the premises at Jordan Place, William worked at Gibraltar Cottage on the Common, and George and James had their manufactory at Hanover Road. Although a descendant credited William with the invention of the mosaic technique, it was George

ABOVE: *Trade card of Edmund Nye, with various Tunbridge ware articles bearing his label: candle-holder, tape-measure, boxes, emery and waxer, and pincushion.*

The Butterfly is a mosaic of twelve thousand pieces of woods in their natural colours.

Name — Vanessa Juliana from Amboyna.

ABOVE: *Work-table, made at Nye's manufactory about 1850.*

LEFT, UPPER: *Trade card supplied with the work-table, with description on reverse in Thomas Barton's handwriting. The butterfly on the lid is the same design as one on the bookstand entered in the Great Exhibition of 1851.*

LEFT, LOWER: *Stationery box with same butterfly on lid.*

28

and James who claimed in a near contemporary advertisement to be 'inventors of the Mosaic Inlaid Ware'. Active for most of the first half of the century, the four brothers had either died or retired by 1850.

FENNER

MOSAIC and INLAID FANCY WOOD FURNITURE, consisting of work, flower, chess, backgammon, quartette, and loo tables; work, card, glove, and letter-boxes; writing desks, dressing cases, tea poys, chests and caddies, work baskets, cabinets, card cases, snuff boxes, cigar cases, toilet cushions, dressing glasses, flower vases and stands, card racks, scent and liqueur cases, hand and fire screens, reading desks and stands, inkstands and trays, sun dials, thermometers in boxes and on pedestals, comb and work trays, watch stands &c. &c. – FENNER and Co., of Mount Ephraim, Tunbridge Wells (Manufacturers to their Majesties and the Royal Family), beg to acquaint the Nobility, Gentry, and others, that they have taken Rooms, 209, Regent-Street, for a short period for the purpose of exhibiting for Sale their exclusive and novel Manufacture, which require only to be seen to be admired. (Advertisement, 1837.)

In another advertisement (Colbran, 1839), Fenner & Company claimed to be 'the oldest and only extensive one in the trade', having on hand 'flower vases, tea caddies and numerous other articles peculiar to their establishment, which they are selling at very reduced prices owing to the introduction of new machinery'. Established in the 1790s, the firm carried on until the retirement of William Fenner in 1840. By the end of the eighteenth century they were producing all sorts of articles 'in the turnery or cabinet line', painted wares and wares 'inlaid with all kinds of French and English Prints, in as elegant a style as any yet manufactured'. With the invention of mosaic decoration, Fenner is said to have purchased frames for his pictures from William Burrows but later manufactured his own mosaic wares.

NYE

For some years at the end of the eight-
eenth century and beginning of the nineteenth, William Fenner was in partnership with James Nye and his son Edmund. On his retirement Edmund Nye took over the old premises on Mount Ephraim. In 1836 the young Thomas Barton, one of Wise's apprentices, had joined the firm; he rapidly became the principal designer and eventually was taken into partnership. Barton is said to have been the first to use Berlin woolwork patterns as designs for Tunbridge ware mosaic; he was responsible for some very fine mosaic and gauge work, including the workbox with a representation of part of the remains of Bayham Abbey, and the bookstand with two inlaid butterflies, displayed by Nye at the Great Exhibition of 1851. Some of his designs for mosaic and marquetry of this period survive.

BARTON

Because a greater number of articles from his workshop are marked, Thomas Barton is probably the best known of all Tunbridge ware manufacturers. Having worked with Edmund Nye for many years as his designer and later partner, shortly before Nye's death in 1863 he took over management of the Mount Ephraim manufactory. As well as mosaic ware of a distinctive character, he also produced marquetry, parquetry and transfer-printed wares. A true craftsman, he took pride in the quality of workmanship, was awarded first prize in the First Class for skilled manufacture at the Tunbridge Wells Industrial Exhibition in 1864, organised the Tunbridge Ware trade exhibition and competition in 1899 and continued to manage the business until his death at the age of eighty-three in 1903.

HOLLAMBY

Coming from a Tunbridge ware manufacturing family, Henry Hollamby was apprenticed to George and James Burrows in 1831 and set up business on his own account about 1842. When the Burrows brothers retired, he took over their showrooms on the Pantiles, purchasing much of their stock in trade; by the 1880s he was the largest manufacturer in the town, employing as many as forty hands in his workshop on the Frant Road. In contrast to Thomas Barton, who retailed

Bonnet stand, stationery box, pin table, box and photograph frame bearing Barton labels; letterhead of Thomas Barton, and portrait photograph of Barton in his aldermanic robes. The unusual pattern on the small box recurs on the Tunbridge ware frame in which was mounted a testimonial of loyalty sent to Queen Victoria on her Diamond Jubilee by the Mayor, Aldermen and Burgesses of Tunbridge Wells in 1897.

only from his own two premises and supplied no hawkers, Hollamby catered also for the wholesale and export markets. Occasionally using other processes, he mainly practised tesellated mosaic techniques and was particularly noted for his production of large blocks with topographical views. When his premises were destroyed by fire in 1891, Hollamby sold whatever stock could be salvaged to Boyce, Brown & Kemp.

BOYCE, BROWN & KEMP

This firm is the only one in existence that brings in the power of the steam engine to do all laborious work in the manufacture of Tonbridge ware. (Advertiser, 1890.)

Thomas Amos Boyce had been in the trade at Tonbridge and James Brown had worked at his father's manufactory for some years before they entered into partnership with John Kemp and set up a Tunbridge ware factory in Camden Road in 1873. Seven years later they acquired the business of James Brown senior, which enabled them to expand. They introduced more mechanisation into the industry but,

apart from a greater use of long rectangular tesserae in their mosaic work, they do not seem to have been responsible for any significant innovation. By 1890 they were producing mosaic views of Eridge Castle, Battle Abbey, Hever and Tonbridge castles, Penshurst Place and the Pantiles, similar to those of Hollamby; possibly one firm supplied the other with designs or blocks. When Hollamby closed following the fire in 1891, Boyce, Brown & Kemp bought up the remaining stock, and on Barton's death in 1903 they became the sole manufacturers of Tunbridge ware. During the First World War James Brown, the last of the original partners, sold out to a John Ellis.

TUNBRIDGE WELLS MANUFAC-TURING COMPANY AND OTHERS

About 1923 the new proprietor of the old firm of Boyce, Brown & Kemp sold the business to David King, who renamed it the Tunbridge Wells Manufacturing Company Limited, 'sole proprietors and manufacturers of Royal Tunbridge Ware'. Unfortunately the ambition to transform it into a national industry that would ap-

LEFT: *Selection of small unmarked articles, known to have been made by Boyce, Brown & Kemp, having belonged to James Hollamby, a former apprentice turner (1878-83).*

BELOW: *Selection of bandings from the workshop of Thomas Green, including some from Boyce, Brown & Kemp and other manufactories.*

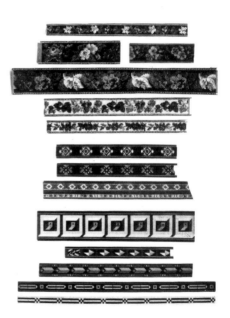

peal to the export market came to nothing, principally because of the unpopularity of the general manager, 'a difficult man of little experience, who alienated the old hands'. By 1926 the last of 'the famous Royal Tunbridge Wells Ware Factories', which had 'produced this unique ware for nearly 300 years', was failing. Meanwhile, Kemp's son had left in disgust and started a new business in Rye, East Sussex; and here during the 1930s there was a brief revival of the industry. In 1931 Thomas Littleton Green of Maidstone moved to Rye, acquired much of the old stock of Boyce, Brown & Kemp and took Richard Kemp into partnership for a time to instruct him in the craft. Slowly the Rye Mosaic Works established itself but came to an end with the Second World War; returning from the forces to find both premises and stock damaged, Green was too disheartened to start afresh. More recently there have been several attempts on the part of individual craftsmen to revive mosaic ware, but on a commercial scale the industry finished with Thomas Green.

As early as the 1880s the decline was recognised and attributed partly to 'the all-round bad times', but also to competition from 'cheap foreign goods without wear or labour in them – painted articles of light make'; in the 1890s it was deplored that the public 'would sooner purchase a box adorned with what is called German strap work, or rough inlaid bands of dyed woods, than they would give perhaps an extra shilling or two for genuine ware'. The labour-intensive industry could not last; Thomas Barton was so perturbed that shortly before his own death he instructed a favourite apprentice: 'My boy, I don't want to lose you but my advice to you is that you get out of this industry at once. It's dying – there is no future.'

PLACES TO VISIT

Intending visitors are advised to find out the times of opening of museums before making a special journey.

Birmingham Museum and Art Gallery (Pinto Collection), Chamberlain Square, Birmingham B3 3DH. Telephone: 0121-235 2834.

Brighton Art Gallery and Museum, 4/5 Pavilion Buildings, Brighton, East Sussex BN1 1EE. Telephone: 01273 603005.

Guildhall Museum, High Street, Rochester, Kent ME1 1PY. Telephone: 01634 848717.

Hove Museum and Art Gallery, 19 New Church Road, Hove, East Sussex BN3 4AB. Telephone: 01273 779410 or 329794. Queen Mary's Collection.

Maidstone Museum and Art Gallery, St Faith's Street, Maidstone, Kent ME14 1LH. Telephone: 01622 754497.

Salisbury and South Wiltshire Museum, The King's House, 65 The Close, Salisbury, Wiltshire SP1 2EN. Telephone: 01722 332151.

Tunbridge Wells Museum and Art Gallery, Civic Centre, Mount Pleasant, Royal Tunbridge Wells, Kent TN1 1JN. Telephone: 01892 526121 or 547221.

Victoria and Albert Museum, Cromwell Road, South Kensington, London SW7 2RL. Telephone: 0171-938 8500.

Worthing Museum and Art Gallery, Chapel Road, Worthing, West Sussex BN11 1HP. Telephone: 01903 239999 extension 2528.

FURTHER READING

Austen, Brian. *Tunbridge Ware and Related European Decorative Woodwares.* W. Foulsham & Co. Ltd, revised edition 1992.

King, K. B. *The Views Illustrated on End Grain Tunbridge Ware Designs* (duplicated typescript). Privately published, 1981.

Pinto, E. H. and E. R. *Tunbridge and Scottish Souvenir Woodware.* G. Bell & Sons, 1970.

Swann, F. 'Introduction' in *Tunbridge Ware – An Exhibition and Sale.* Sotheby's Belgravia, 1980.

Younghusband, E. *Mansions, Men and Tunbridge Ware.* The Windsor Press, 1949.

Bracelet of palmyra, brooches (pansy brooch probably by Thomas Barton), hat pin by Boyce, Brown & Kemp, shawl pin, cuff links, reticule bar, papier mâché spectacles case, turned ebony beads and cross said to have been made by George Wise.